Copyright © 2018 Dionna Walker
All rights reserved.

No part of this publication may be reproduced, distributed, or transmitted in any form or by any means, including photocopying, recording, or other electronic or mechanical methods, without the prior written permission of the publisher, except in the case of brief quotations embodied in critical reviews and certain other noncommercial uses permitted by copyright law.

For permission visit
Author Website www.BusinessMomInc.Com

ISBN: 10:1724927477
ISBN-13:978-1724927477

DEDICATION

I Dedicate This Book To

My Family

Husband

& Children

Cordell Jr

Jeremiah

Jarell

Candace

Johnathan

Alonna

CONTENTS

THE MOMMY HUSTLE
DS WALKER

CHAPTER

1. Let's Get Real 1
2. Finding Your Purpose 3
3. You Are Not Cinderella 6
4. Support System 9
5. Determination 11
6. Confident Woman 14
7. Momtrepreneur 18
8. Beastly Hustle 20
9. Boss Mom 23
10. The Hustle 28

The Mommy Hustle Diary 35

CHAPTER ONE:
LET'S GET REAL

1
Let's Get Real

The Journey of Motherhood has been like a fast Moving rolling coaster, at Times Scary. But never Without Excitement And Thrills. Some Women have had the luxury of being prepared and stable before having their first child however , I couldn't relate. I had my first son at 15, and later in life have had more. This blessing and my new life at 15 really changed the way I, looked at life moving forward. I, could no longer relate to being out of Control, the partying and regular teenage drama. I had to grow up and do it fast. I felt like I was being accelerated from normal teenager to a Woman that only option was to provide. But only by the grace of God, I made it this far.

The Moment I became a Mother, all my dreams and goals for myself were no longer as important, All I wanted was to be the best mother and parent I could be. Even now, this is still my desire, but it has taken me so much effort that at times, it seems to have brought me to my breaking point. I so desperately needed to find my voice back then and believe that I was enough. Even enough to be a Business Woman.

Mothers get so caught up in taking care of homes and children, that we forget to take the time to do things we Enjoy. I so desperately needed to find my identity again, besides just "A Mom" I always Wanted to be in business for myself, but often put it off because I didn't think I could do it or have time for it. Starting a new business while going after my dreams was very hard for me initially. I couldn't find the time to do what I needed to do to be successful at both simultaneously. I eventually learned that time management and dedication would play a major part if I wanted to be successful.

I began to spend less time on things that didn't add any value to my life or goals, and more time doing things that would. Eventually, I realized all the extra BS was just that, Bullshit.

1
Let's Get Real

Motherhood, which has been the best thing that could have ever happened to me, has pushed me into following my dreams. I am now a better person and mother, who can now better manage stress, family, and responsibilities.

The person I have become is so much more powerful, focused, stronger, and ready to take on any and all challenges ahead. Motherhood has brought me Face-To-Face with my Truth. I had to really tap into myself; I had to Find my Voice. This has taken a lot of work up to this point, but I had quickly realized back in the day that I was actually capable of starting my own business and finding my purpose all while being a Great Daughter, Mother, sister and Wife.

CHAPTER TWO:
FINDING YOUR PURPOSE

2
Finding Your Purpose

Your purpose is the reason why you exist it's the reason for being. Finding your life purpose is very much about finding yourself. Life with a purpose drives you when you wake up each morning. For so long my only purpose in life was solely all about my family. from the moment I woke until the last sentence in my kids bedtime stories. I use to be the mother who sat and wondered what was my purpose in life? I mean, besides being a Mother and I couldn't come up with anything. In that moment I begin to work on doing things to better myself as a Mother and businesswoman.

I did not want to be on my dying bed regretting not living my life to the fullest so I changed my mindset and goals. Day by day I did something to change my lifestyle.

Where do you start when everything is against you?
Easy. Just start don't allow procrastination get in your way!
Success is yours as long as you believe in fully living out your life purpose.

I believed that owning a business was my life purpose I didn't like waking up every morning going to a job I really hated. I begin to really think about what I wanted to accomplish out of life. I made it my mission to start Making a list of everything I liked and love to do. I made sure not to waste my time on things that didn't serve a purpose. in today generation it is so easy to become distracted especially with electronics and everything being so instant. if I was spending my time on a task it had to be for a purpose or reason. ASK YOURSELF WHAT DO YOU NEED TO BE SUCCESSFUL IN YOUR BUSINESS?

To find your purpose is to find yourself and self analyzing who you truly are. Becoming an Entrepreneur not only tested my purpose in life but my faith.

2
Finding Your Purpose

Building a business can cause an increasing amount of stress without a strong support system. It is very important to gather your support system and keep them close. Surround yourself around people that will help your business and you reach full potential.

Nothing is impossible! to be a stay at home mom or business mom is to be undervalued by society. To be happy and a successful you must believe that what you do is beneficial to you and your family. It must serve a purpose. The same goes for entrepreneurs.
In the beginning it's a challenge just to believe in your dream I've learned to stand up and advocate for what you believe in.

Many people want to become an entrepreneur but only few recognize early that building a business can cause an increasing amount of stress especially for stay at home moms or single mothers.

The beginner entrepreneur has no clue where to start and at times, seeks the advice of seasoned entrepreneurs. However, an average seasoned entrepreneur may not or will not share resources or give advice, fearful that you may succeed beyond them. Many entrepreneurs start a business for a chance at career freedom or to become the master of their own destinies. Others are looking for alternative income opportunities to supplement their already existing careers and/or life.

Do you believe that starting your own business is your life purpose?
Can you see yourself doing this your entire Life?

Below are 5 questions to help you think more about your life purpose.

2
Finding Your Purpose

Answer the questions after thoughtfully pondering them.

1. What kind of person are you?

2. What do you love to do?

3. What are some reasons behind your passion?

4. What do you want or need to be successful?

5. How do you think success would change you?

PURPOSE FINDING EXERCISE

1. Write it out-write down 10 things you admire about yourself.
2. Childhood Dreams-Think about what you wanted to be when you grew up.
3. Who do you admire, who are your heroes
4. Create a quite space.
5. Find and seek out your fears.
6. Seek advice from professionals and trusted friends
7. Communicate with like minded individuals

CHAPTER **THREE**:
YOU ARE NOT CINDERELLA

3
You Are Not Cinderella

There comes a time when you just have to say Fuck it! Things will not always go the way you want it to and that's okay. Ladies were not Cinderella its okay to just relax, yes! I said, it Relax! Step away from the cleaning and put down the power kitchen cooking tools. As, I am writing this my son is tugging my shirt to look for a car he lost for the 100th time today.

Taking a moment to relax can allow you to get things done that are really important to your goals and business.

Its okay to remove the superhero cape. We are not perfect we are Mothers trying our best to provide for our family and we too require a break. Finding the time to really focus on myself required tons of practice and planning. I live by a daily schedule to insure for about one hour is me time. It could be anything from reading a book, listening to music, burning your favorite candles, or even a bubble bath. I use this time to hit the restart button. motherhood is very overwhelming and can be stressful if you allow it to be. My children is my entire life and in order for me to be at my best taking a break is a must.

How Do You unwind?

Motherhood requires a lot I can hug, kiss, play in makeup, enjoy the video game with my boys even read tons of books I've read over-and-Over. But let's be Real MOMMA NEEDS A BREAK!

How do you recharge?

Every day I take 25 minutes, in my free space, to pray and ask God for strength. I read in my free space and maybe drink a glass of wine while I relax. I do this sometimes during lunch or even after. I shut off my phone and really enjoy my quiet time.

3
You Are Not Cinderella

Sometimes you get so caught up trying to build our empire that you forget to just take a moment to relax. Taking a moment to unwind can help you come up with business ideas or professional goals. Surrounding your free space with milestone you accomplished could be good for encouragements. I challenge you to take a moment out your day to just praise yourself for all your accomplishments.

Finding your free space

Do you have a "space" in your home where you can unwind, listen to music or even read a book.

This area must be stress free and work free. This is your calm place for meditation and prayer. In my free space I pray and ask GOD for strength. I read in my free space maybe drink a glass of wine and relax. Sometimes you get so caught up trying to build our empire we forget to just take a moment to relax. II challenge you to take a moment out your day to just praise yourself for all your accomplishments. This book is a tool for you to write down ideas or even Business Goals.

Can you set aside time to just relax?

Most Business owners are so stressed and overwhelmed relaxing can help you not burn out. Everyday I would like 25 minutes to pray and relax sometimes during lunch or even after. I would shut off my phone and really enjoy my quiet time. Find your free space and enjoy it.

Mothers we allow ourselves to become extremely overwhelmed With guilt. If our home is not perfect we feel as if we're failing. I tried to be the perfect wife, mother, sister, and business woman this just added extra unwanted stress. I wanted to be perfect and I expected everyone and everything around me to be the same way.

3
You Are Not Cinderella

This kinda mindset will only burn you out. It's okay to just let things take it natural course in life. Taking a moment to relax allowed me to approach things with a clear head and appreciate my success It's okay to take a break.

Do you ever reconsider rejuvenating Your business idea to birth a different outcome? Just like our skin and everything else we too needs to be rejuvenated. We need to start fresh with ideas and approaches for our business. The Moment I rejuvenated my mindset business became stress free.

Are you rejuvenated?

Have you rejuvenated your mindset?

Steps to Relax

1. Find a quiet room to pray or relax
2. Read a book
3. Focus on your spiritual life
4. Set goals and work to achieve them
5. Plan a dinner with friends or love partner
6. Plan a day for just yourself
7. Do things you truly love
8. Relax
9. Remove stress from your life.

CHAPTER **FOUR:**
SUPPORT SYSTEM

4
Support System

I use to be the victim of meeting other peoples expectations. I strived to seem cool amongst my peers I did all sorts of extra things to try and make my parents and family happy. I felt the need to be favored among my colleagues.

This type of energy to be the BEST or be LIKED was draining.
when I started worrying about myself and grinding 24/7 for my own pleasures attracted the right type of people. I stopped being extra and the right tribe of people came to me. our time together is not forced because we choose to work together or support each other.

A mommy hustler is someone who don't let life get the best of her. Mothers put so much on the line for our children because we want them to be better than we are or experience more out of life. This requires support.

Do you have a village of people that supports you?
Not everyone can or will understand your passion in your business. Not everyone will support you!
It's vital to figure out who your supporters are.

A supporter will be there to offer you great advice. He or she is not afraid to let you know when you are wrong and will tell you the truth despite your feelings. This person will go the extra mile to help you succeed. If you surround yourself around followers, please make room for your supporters.

Here are a few questions that can help you identify your support system.
1. Are you surrounding yourself around positive energy?
2. Can you identify positive energy in your life?
3. Are you surrounding yourself around positive people?
4. Who are the positive people in your life?
5. Can you identify the positive people in your life?
6. How are they impacting you to become better?
7. Who is your support system?

4
Support System

Surround yourself around people that will help you reach your goals in your life whether big or small. Find people that are already in positions where you want to be and not around people that have never accomplished anything or who aren't going anywhere. Surround yourself around people that have made accomplishments and going somewhere in life.

Write down five people who will support you no matter win or lose. These people are not afraid to tell you when you're wrong and are there to help you development.

1.

2.

3.

4.

5.

When things aren't going well or when you are just not feeling that great, support and encouragement is a necessity. For those who try to tough it alone, it can be a difficult, uphill battle.

Finding a mentor who has a lot of wisdom, experience and insight. This can also be found in friends, family or colleagues who have experienced running a business first-hand.

Before we get to the point of great difficulty, which is when you want to give up or are feeling overwhelmed to the point of quitting, or in anticipation of life's little setbacks, we should implement strategies or have a support system in place to help us through some of those rough spots.

CHAPTER **FIVE:**
DETERMINATION

5
Determination

When I began this business journey so many people around me didn't support me in the beginning. most Business Moms go thru this journey alone sometimes the people close to you will not be the ones who takes you to the next level. The success of your business is not about who support you. it's about how will you proceed after your closet family or friends look past your business.

My biggest mistake in business is expecting my family or friends to support my business. I learned that people will support you when They are Good and Ready. I appreciate my Family and friends who invest in my business and you will also!

In Mommy World things get hard, you start thinking that it's not worth it and that you just want to let it go! but let me tell you this, the more pain and suffering you put into something, the better it'll feel when you accomplish the goal.

How to gain determination
Determination is inside all of us but we just have to find it. We must have the willpower to accomplish any and everything we set out to do. Have you ever wanted something so bad as a child you talked about it all the time and ask your parents to buy it and you wouldn't let up until you receive it? That's what I call determination. I see it everyday with my children. Not letting up and asking for help to achieve your goals are required tasks. We all have practiced determination at some point in our lives so look deep and continue to be determined in whatever you are doing.

How to use determination

Determination is considered a laudable and coveted personality trait because it indicates that individuals are motivated to succeed, which translates to them getting tasks done and accomplishing goals.

5
Determination

Sacrifices of determination.
Determination means you look at yourself and you find no excuses. And when you find your strengths and weaknesses, you better utilize them and accomplish everything you have in mind with no excuses. If you fail, don't worry about it. Just get right back up and continue. If you don't fail, then you're not doing anything right and are afraid of failing. Failing is something you cannot ignore. It's something everyone comes across in life. That's why people learn from mistakes and move on.

The only person holding you back is you and your thoughts.

Typically, the term procrastination carries a negative tone and is often used in describing delays. For me, procrastination means taking too much time to make the very best decisions for my business. Sometimes this will result in losing a partner or not meeting marketing deadlines. The amount of time you spend making a decision for your business operations could either benefit or defeat your goals. You always want to practice patience and discipline in business and never jump head first! Take your time and decide which business deal to take on first and then do not procrastinate.

How to identify procrastination?

Sometimes procrastination takes place until the last minute before a deadline needs to be met. It can take hold of any aspect of your life such as putting off cleaning the stove, repairing a leaky roof, or even visiting the doctor or dentist. It can also lead to feelings of guilt, inadequacy, depression and self-doubt.

To help procrastination, break large tasks down into smaller, more manageable ones.

For example, the big task of getting new representation can seem overwhelming.

5
Determination

Divide the workload and give yourself small, specific tasks with deadlines to help you create an action-oriented plan. One day you might research offices that are accepting submissions. The next day you might ask friends for referrals. The following day you compose your cover letter, and so on. Remind yourself that there's always more to be done than can be done. Always ask yourself if you're getting the most important things done before the least important.

Below are ways to avoid procrastination.

1. Stop thinking too much
2. Stop wasting time thinking of all the things that could go wrong and just begin
3. Prepare
4. Set daily goals for your business to accomplish them. If you need to create a Facebook business page, set a few hours aside to get it done. If you need printed material, hire someone.
5. Have faith
   Faith is taking the first step even when you don't see the whole staircase.
6. Set goals
   Goal setting is the first step in turning the invisible into visible.
7. Make a decision
   A day is made of hundreds of small decisions so don't agonize over what to do. Decisions force us to close the door on other possibilities and continue to move forward.
8. Face your fear
   Never give up and continue to push forward.
   Practice taking the next step

CHAPTER SIX:
CONFIDENCE WOMAN

6
Confidence Woman

Gaining Confidence while building on Your business

Working next to the top businesses or organizations in the city. I begin to question my abilities. I wondered how i got to this high place in my business. Then i had to remind myself i'm in this position because of my hard work and dedication. I applied myself just like everyone else and I was in certain situations because of my accomplishments. Moving forward my confidence begin to show thru my public speeches and conversations. I often felt bad because i was surrounded by people with degrees and college experiences i felt like i couldn't carry on a conversation with a college graduates without feeling stupid .. I went back to school college not to prove something to anyone else but to make myself feel better about me.

What is confidence?
The feeling or belief that one can rely on someone or something.

How to gain confidence?

Package yourself for success develop your brand. Be a great communicator look and act confident When you look the part, you'll carry yourself with more confidence. Be physically active in all BUSINESS aspects Do your best and worry less Let go of small mistakes. Continue to grow and improve. Write down your business goal and look at them daily. Be determined and negotiate fearlessly failure is an event not a person. Believe in yourself know when to focus and when to multitask.

How to use confidence.

Confidence in yourself, others, and in business is vital to your success. If you are thinking of starting a business or you already own a business, you must already have some self confidence to take such a big risk.

6
Confidence Woman

Having the Tools, resources, and guidance is important When starting your business. I reached out to so many People and Most of the woman I came into contact with helped out a lot But, a few was bit by the jealous bug and caused unwanted Drama.

"SOME"woman in business we're nasty, jealous, mean, and shady.

I remember a lady who canceled a meeting I was hosting for a major community event just to be nasty about me not accepting a Business Collaboration. I didn't allow others insecurities stop me from being great. I became confident and bold in my decision making when it came to working and collaborating my business. Even at my early stages in business I chose who I wanted work with. Not all women in business are Nasty. God sent me some powerful mentors and business partners. I am thankful that I spotted the snakes early on in business.

When I hear women empowerment all I can think about is what happens after the empowerment is over? What are you doing to hold yourself accountable?

Confidence is a major key factor in business you must be confident in yourself. Entrepreneurs deal with a lot so carry yourself with confidence. You got this.

Let me tell you! Some people are afraid of change or something new. They are afraid to let go and take a chance. There is great power in not knowing what happens next. The moment I decided to leave my job and stop helping build someone else's empire, I began to walk into my purpose. Are you determined to secure the future you want to live? Are you ready to step out on faith?

6
Confidence Woman

What is "Speaking into existence?"

When you claim greatness into existence over your life, you're claiming good things to happen. Maybe you are seeking a new job, car, house or even a marriage. Claiming good things over your life helps put positive vibes out into the universe.

Everything I speak out into the universe becomes mine. Speak good over your life! There are enough people doubting you and your abilities so always speak greatness over your life. Speaking this into existence is just the first step. You must take action and work hard to secure the lifestyle you want to live. This requires much determination.

Stepping out on faith and taking a risk can be fearful and scary but sometimes you just have to go for it.

Here are three simple questions that helped me step out on faith.

1. Are you worried about paying bill's? Great! Step out on faith.

One day I was in my tub thinking about what people would say about me at my funeral and what I had done worth remembering? Then, I focused my attention on all the great things I wanted to do. That's when, day-by-day, I began to not worry about bills or money. I decided to step out on faith and began to do what I wanted with no hesitation.

2. Are you worried about how you're going to send your kids to college? Good! Step out on faith. What are you doing today to secure your children's futures? When given the opportunity to work extra hours or gain increases in income, do you take it? For every penny you earn, 10% of it should go toward your children's future! Stop worrying and step out on faith!

6
Confidence Woman

3. Tired of your boss treating you like crap? Wonderful. Step out on faith. Many people live life doing just enough to get by, which can lead to a very miserable future. You should always want more. Never feel obligated to stay in a situation just because you are barely getting by.

As I stated earlier, speaking good over my life wasn't enough. Stepping out on faith HAVING CONFIDENCE and applying myself was what I needed too. My determination to win was now at a whole new level as I spoke success into my life.

So…….

If you want a new job, Have Confidence and speak it into existence.

If you want a fast new car, speak it into existence.

If you want to find a husband or wife, speak it into existence.

Always speak good things into your life.

CHAPTER SEVEN:
MOMTREPRENEUR

7
Momtrepreneur

Momtrepreneur is a mother who owns a business to earn extra income without the commitment of traditional employment!

Most of us often work from home, especially at the beginning stages of building a Business. Typically our duties consist of balancing the responsibilities of home life, work life and everything in between–from one location. (My Bed) or basically anywhere my kids haven't been.

Being a business mom alone tends to put a sour taste in the closed minds mouth. We often face obstacles the average person will face in business. But the difference is when our kids or home are in shambles we don't stop being in business we dealt with just about any and everything that could go wrong from the experience of being a mom.

Entrepreneurship leaves little time for the luxury of a normal life such as family dinners, social life, normal sleep, or exercise. let alone the responsibilities of being a mother and wife.

Yet everyday I pull this impossible task off by managing my time spending it with the people who matters the most to me. My family.

No. managing a business and motherhood isn't easy and I never neglect my children or husband I manage my time. Finding Balance between "Business Mom" and Just being "mom".

Being a mother I have developed a skill set that includes content switching multitasking and having knowledge of what actually is going on in the next room just by listening.

You got this!

7
Momtrepreneur

How to manage your time and not procrastinate!

1. Don't spend unnecessary time on things that will not benefit your business.

2. Plan out your work week! I like to write down everything I need to do for my business in my Daily accountability planner.

3. Execute Everything off your list don't overthink it. Overthinking will only distract you from getting the job done. If you miss something or make a mistake it's okay. Move on to something else. Just don't give up.

4. Worry less.

5. Every mistake is a Lesson! If you stress over it you will miss the lesson. Learn from your mistakes and get better.

6. Lastly, make time for your babies and family!

CHAPTER EIGHT:
BEASTLY HUSTLE

8
Beastly Hustle

The mom who hustles is someone who fearlessly, Beastly and relentlessly goes after the life she want not allowing negativity Society Her past or negative energy get in her way.

She has faith, determination, courage, and knows that opportunities are something she has to create herself. Hustling isn't easy but the Beast in me makes my mommy hustle worth the risk.

I'm still learning! but what I know for sure is when I apply these 5 things I listed below to my everyday, "Mommy Hustle" it has undoubtedly made a difference in my success.

Be a coachable person.
Be a Positive person.
Celebrate accomplishments.
Accept help.
Accept and trust others.

Let's face it: even if you consider yourself "super mom," you'll need a little bit of assistance.

There are many places I could have to turn for help. But being the amateur person I once was I took it upon myself to carry this load of Entrepreneurship on my own. and that was the stupidest and by far the worst business move I made. You can't manage a business alone your going to need some type of assistance. But you have to be able to Trust people to take over or lead. I had to fix something within myself in order to allow other people to help me. This required me to make a few adjustments with self. Finding the right help is important and setting your mindset to really appreciate help from other can be hard but you can't run a successful business alone. Think for a minute and ask yourself what would make the perfect assistant or business partner? Now get ready for what is next.
It's time to hold ourselves accountable.

8
Beastly Hustle

Accountability
There comes a time when you have to stop sleeping on yourself, stop settling, stop trying to fit in, and stop being afraid of the outcome, You must hold yourself accountable. Stop with the excuses and go after what you want. Unapologetically do what is best for you! Don't let anyone tell you what you deserve, Don't let anyone tell you what you can't do. In this season, we are taking accountability seriously!

Throughout my life I always had a hard time trusting people something within me always stated that people wanted to take things from me or use me for personal gain. And then I asked myself just what the hell could a person gain from me? Like why am I so guarded when it comes to other people? I had my fair share of being used and abused by people I think my early independence in life lead me to hold a guard up with me from the fear of being disappointed or let down if I expected too much. I taught myself to always keep a constant guard up even with close friends I never let anyone truly into my Zone. But once I started my business I had to Work with other I had to communicate and share myself with other. I wanted to carry the mindset of I can do it alone I don't need nobody and that's the worse mindset to have in business. I had to use that negative energy and turn it into a positive.

Stop and consider for a moment reasons why you don't like someone. Maybe you think he or she is greedy and selfish. Or possibly, their dismissive nature to others and yourself can be downright mean. In other words, there are some character flaws or disagreeable traits in others that can bother and irritate you.

Can you get past these issues to get the job done?
Learning to get past difficult people will keep you in business for a very long time. As a professional, you have to be able to handle yourself in difficult situations.

8
Beastly Hustle

I typically go into a business partnership knowing the risks. I usually reach out to businesses I can help or receive help from. For me, each person I work with can add to my business rather than take away.

In business, your name is like credit. Businesses love doing credibility check. This is when someone ask around about you in regards to your personality, business partnerships, ethics, and many more. Do you have good credit? Getting into a relationship with businesses that don't have a credit can hurt your new business. Tread lightly when you partner with other businesses. Always do your homework!

During my first year of my business, before I jumped into a partnership, I did my homework. I only had 3 partners with other organizations. Each partnership brought different things to the table that I couldn't provide. I really had to accept the fact that I wasn't the know-it-all that I thought I was. Reaching out to these individuals and accepting I couldn't do it all was a major step in my business development. Now, not only are things running a lot more smoothly for my business, but I have helped other businesses reach their goals, gain exposure and build new partnerships.

Not blaming yourself or feeling down because of a partnership or business deal didn't work out is very important. Learn from it and apply the changes to your next business deal. Sometimes it's not your fault. Maybe the business you're partnering with could have issues with your business or getting into a partnership all together. Just be aware and learn as much as you can about the businesses you are trying to partner with. Never allow negative feelings get in the way of you achieving your goals. Sometimes you just have to bite the bullet, stay determined, and go after your goals.

CHAPTER NINE:
BOSS MOM

9
Boss Mom

What would you consider a boss mom?

Do you know your business Market?

When beginning my business journey my Target market was pitched to Mothers Because I knew these ladies were serious and had no time for error. I knew my market was full of hard working women who has been told they couldn't do it and is in need of guidance and support. I work with women who was looking for a new life after divorce trying to pick up the pieces or the stripper who is saving tips to open her bakery. I could relate to my market I too am a mother and I know the struggles of being a boss mom.

A life without challenge hardships or purpose is pointless with challenges comes strength self confidence and growth. Too many people wants to fast track to success but miss the point of really getting it out the mud grinding and working hard.

What is your heart like?

When you reach that "BOSS MOM" Status are you able to respect or help others trying to reach your leave of success? So many times I see entrepreneurs upset or affected by individuals coming to them for business advice. at some point we're all beginners at something there are ways to help other without giving resources away for free!

Here are 5 tips to offer business advice without giving away free advice

Ask they would like to set up a consultation.
Direct them to someone who could offer better advice.
Refer them to an Author or book that could help guide them.
Offer advice to where they can search about Entrepreneurship.
Trade service for advice.

9
Boss Mom

Remain humble and no we don't work for free but every opportunity is an amazing opportunity to level up your business.

What is Your Heart Like?
Yes , I just asked you... WHAT IS YOUR HEART LIKE??

What type of person are you ?
What type of mindset do you carry around?
Do you treat people how you wanted to be treated in business?
Do you overlook people because you share a different lifestyle?

In business leave that judgement mindset to society we're working hard to break down barriers. Whether you're a janitor or riches ceo treat everyone with respect.

What type of Boss are You?
Do you treat Others well?
Can you handle being in a position of Power?

My children tells me everyday mom when you yell or scream will that help you get things done at work? And I thought for a moment that I don't have to yell or scream to make people do what I want them too. just because I hold this Title doesn't mean I have to be this person in charge all the time holding this big high title. This type of BOSSY energy will follow you and It followed into my home instead of being understanding and considerate of my surroundings I was Bossy 24-7.

My children and husband didn't deserve this type of Energy yesss I'm the Founder ceo And Author but when I'm home I need to be a Mother and wife. I had to learn how to distance mom from, "BossMom". My children just wanted Mom the person who pops popcorn and watch movies in our matching pjs. They wanted mom who colored painted and did fun activity with.

9
Boss Mom

My business and clients deserved the BOSS who works very hard. My clients deserved the Boss who carried herself with confidence and some they can trust me with their dreams and vision to get the job done. I had to check myself and you will need to do that a lot in business to reach the next level in success. When you level up your business will grow. And when you fail there is Growth their too! you learn for failure.

Can you deal with Rejection?
If you deal with rejection personally, you'll struggle to grow your business.

If you can get past the possibilities of a rejection from a potential date, job opportunity, bank, or business deal, then you can look at every "no" as one step closer to that "yes". Instead of getting defeated by rejection, learn to see it as just one step on the path to your ultimate goal.

Received a rejection? Ask questions regarding the decision. Sample questions can include "Can you share advice on how I can improve my business proposal?" and "Why is my business not a good fit for your business?" Listen carefully to their responses and encourage them to be completely honest with their feedback. One of the most important things to do in business is to listen and learn to ask questions. Ultimately, thank the person or company for their time and consideration and leave on a positive note.

Once you have taken their feedback into consideration, assess any problem areas and make changes within your business and adjust your approach as needed. You'll likely find that you get fewer "no's" and more "yeses" however rejection can be hard. No one likes to be rejected. Rejection will never disappear without making necessary adjustments. Facing rejection doesn't make you a failure but failing to learn from them just might! However, a "no" can mean "I don't know?" or "I'm not ready at the moment." and in these type of situations, leave your contact information and thank them.

9
Boss Mom

I remember one time, a business swore against accepting new clients. However, by the end of the week, the business called and offered us a business partnership and we were added to their list and moved ahead of every other business. How did I do it? I left the meeting asking and answering questions. I also left my contact information behind so they could contact me. Never leave a stone unturned.

Ask questions:
"Why can't we work together?"

"Does my business not fit into your business partnership agendas?"
"Do you see something within my business plan that worries you?"
Leave contact information
Leaving a business card behind is not only professional, but a great way to easily provide information about yourself without coming off aggressive. Maturity is when you realize that getting rejected isn't always a bad thing. I am thankful for every employer that said no to me. It is my prayer that I walk into all that I am called to be and do so that I can turn around and be a financial blessing to others. I am thankful for the rejections. Embrace your failures as one step closer to accomplishing your goals! Don't take rejection as you if you have failed. Make changes and apply it to your business so it can continue to grow.

Always be prepared for the possibility of a no. If you are, then you will do the follow:
1. Leave your contact information
2. Ask questions
3. Learn from your mistakes
4. Take into consideration the answers you received from asking why the company didn't want to do business with you.
5. Work on your deliverance.
6. Prepare for better business opportunities.

9
Boss Mom

Having the right attitude about a "no" can really go a long way. It can actually get you closer to getting a "yes". You must fail in order to win. In business, you might get a 100 "no's" but once you get that one "yes", you will feel more successful today then you were yesterday!

Remember to ask questions when faced with rejection. Ask yourself, "What can I do to secure the next business deal?" If you hear "no" a lot, it's probably a hint to fix something with your strategies. Always ask questions to know what to fix and update for the next time. Always learn from feedback, apply it, and get back out there

CHAPTER TEN:
THE HUSTLE

10
The Hustle

The Reason why I choose to work with moms is because I understand and get their struggles. Being a mommy hustler requires a tremendous amount of self-Motivation resources and Support! When it all boils down to the success of your business you must be extremely self motivated you are the boss, so reassurance and positive feedback comes from your willpower to not give up when things goes Wrong. You must have a strong clear and positive mindset

Do you have a unmistakable and relentless" Mommy Hustle" Mentalities?

Being optimistic allowed me to have the ability to move past my own comfort zone. I believed I can succeed no matter what. Even when nobody showed up to my Event leaving me with a room full of vendor and myself Even when I wasted Money hosting events and nobody supporting with so many people and negative energy against Me I believed in my success. My spiritual relationship with god me to meditate and pray over my business to manifest. Find peace and relaxation to be the best you be for your business.

Are You ready for THE HUSTLE?

Who do your hustle consist of?

Who are you Hustling For?

When I begin this hustling journey I had to eliminate everything and everybody that was getting into the way of My Hustle. Anything that affects my growth and ability to succeed was not worth my time I did not spend countless of hours on The Social media and other distractions. I spend my time on things that will help me reach my reasoning behind my hustling. When you feel like your wasting time ask yourself what type of value is this adding to my life? Will this add value to my life?

10
The Hustle

I'm hustling for financial freedom generational wealth I'm hustling to show all the little girls in the hood you don't have to become A Product of your Environment.

Are you in position to reach the next level in your life and business? So many entrepreneurs have Avery hard time positioning their business to reach target markets or reaching it full potential because they don't know where to start I will provide information tools and resources to help you jumpstart your business.

What type of person are you?

Answering these questions will help you self analysis what type of entrepreneur you are!

1. Are you self motivated?
2. Do you have passion?
3. Do you have a plan?
4. Are you innovative?
5. Are you optimistic?
6. Do you have social media skills?
7. Do you have money management skills?
8. Are you organized?
9. Do you trust others working for your business?
10. How do you deal with rejection?

Below you will find ways I used social media and marketing tools to become a successful business.

I share a few of these tips in many of my publications and Articles here you can have full access for your personal use!!

10
The Hustle

" The Hustle "

1. GRAPHIC DESIGNER- Graphic designing has become a part of every industry. Graphic designers produce the visual media that business need to brand, promote and market. Hiring a good graphic designer is key to success so make sure you do your research. Once you find your designer, begin to design your logo. This will get the attention of customers and potential business partners. Once you hire your Graphic designer begin to promote yourself in different ways. You can purchase T-shirts with your logo or place it on other material. Encourage family members and friends to support you in your efforts with your business. Have them help you promote your business by passing out informational flyers or purchase banners and place them around.

Do you know The Difference between BRAND vs. Branding
2. Brand is not branding. The difference between brand and branding is that one is a marketing tool and the other is an action. Branding is about defining, while advertising is about promoting. A brand is a person's emotional response -a gut feeling about an organization, a product, or a service. In essence, your customers own your brand, you do not. You don't have direct control of the perceptions held by customers.

Branding is not about stamping a trademark on everything, but guiding and managing relationships with your customers. You're branding yourself right now as an individual part of the family collective and your business. Realize that you only have partial control of the perceptions with your branding activities.

How Do you use your Facebook?
3. Create your Facebook business page and include information about your business, mission and services you provide. Encourage friends and family to share and like your page. Introduce your business to other organizations or businesses online and like their stuff.

10
The Hustle

My daily goals for Facebook are to share my business page 3 times a day in the morning, at lunch, and around dinnertime. I did the routine for 6 months and received 7 new follower a day. Facebook shouldn't be your only marketing platform. Donors and sponsors will not take you seriously if this is your only source to the world. Get up and Get off "the book."

Hire Website Developers So many Entrepreneurs want to handle all aspects of the business when you can hire someone who can do the job professionally!

Find a company that will develop a website that will cater to your business needs and express your target audience to them.

Make sure your website is:
1. Sleek
2. Modern
3. Safe and secure
4. Include details about the business and owner
5. Blogging - This is a great way to keep traffic coming to your website

Make sure you upkeep your website. This is essential. Customers hate a complicated website. If you become to busy to maintain your website, hire help!

Handwrite Letters
5. People never really handwrite letters now a days. With all the different forms of communication like apps and texting, who has time to write a well-written, signed and sealed letter? We received a response from each hand-written letter we sent. We even closed major business deal and Gained many business sponsorships.

10
The Hustle

Personal Phone Calls
6. Social media Shouldn't be your only connection you have to your customers. Yes! I make follow up phone calls and send text messages. Sometimes people just need that extra push to seal the deal.

I LOVE social media but it's not my only Marketing platform. As an Entrepreneur we must use every trick in the book. I love using old school marketing tools to promote my business.

Here are a few:

Phone Calls

Billboards

Public Transportation

Handwritten Letters

Do what you must to reach your Target Market.

There will come a Time where you have to Present your business to investor or potential clients here are a few ways I mastered this Tasked.

Your business pitch is a presentation by one or more people to an investor or group of investors. You will not get good at pitching unless you experience it first-hand. No one can prepare you for what investors might do or say unless of course, you're psychic! Each business situation is different and you don't want to cheat yourself or your business!

Develop your pitch based on your needs to gain investors. Before you pitch your business to an investor, you must develop what you need and why this investor should help you.

10
The Hustle

During my very first pitch, I was unsure of myself and my business needs. My body language and presentation showed just how naive and unprepared I was. Investors hate to have their time wasted. Take time to prepare your pitch for your business and do your homework for investors. Google will be your best friend as you search for how to create your pitch and on your search for an investor. It is worth your time!

This is the part of the book where I have to just tell it like it is! You can't practice a pitch! Why you ask? Well, every investor is different. One investor might like a video presentation and will you be prepared if all you brought was a graph and outline to the meeting? Learn what your investors like and even if you have to, research the business and call and ask the assistant or secretary for help. Do your homework!

You can practice a million times but that will not help if your investor is not interested in what you're pitching! Trust me, they have heard it all before. Investors want you to tell them why you want their money! This is your chance to sell your business to an investor. Make sure you know how to approach the situation. I'm not suggesting for you to not develop a pitch. I'm suggesting you make sure your pitch is suitable for different types of situations!

Step to developing a perfect pitch!

1. Know exactly what you want and need from investors! Be very upfront about your intentions.

2. Why is your business worth investing in? At this point you should describe your business as if it's the last business on Earth.

3. Always prepare to explain your business to any audience.

10
The Hustle

The hustle is so Real and the struggle along the journey will define the person you really are. Either you fold under pressure or you will boss up become serious about your hustle start learning and becoming the best in your industry.

I encourage YOU to go hard at your MOMMY HUSTLE go after everything they said you couldn't have remain humble and FLEX on your business growth Flex on your business product and flex during your down and Winning season because you have worked hard to get to where you are   that is all the reason to celebrate. Nobody Hustle like a mommy Hustler because her Determination to succeed is unimaginable.

Keep hustling Mommy's!

The Mama Hustle Diary

This book details steps I took to eliminate stress from my life and business. I pray that this Journal helps you on your journey to success!

I challenge you to stay open to your own thoughts and how they impact your feelings towards learning more about your life's purpose.

I Dare you to acknowledge any negative energy as a source to positive energy.

I Dare you to be bold and confident. This diary is for you to create your very own Journey to success.

Date:

Affirmation:

Who or what inspired you today?

Goals:

Business   Personal   Weekly

Weekly Quote:

Date:

Affirmation:

Who or what inspired you today?

Goals:

Business   Personal   Weekly

Weekly Quote:

Date:

Affirmation:

Who or what inspired you today?

Goals:

Business   Personal   Weekly

Weekly Quote:

Date:

Affirmation:

Who or what inspired you today?

Goals:

Business   Personal   Weekly

Weekly Quote:

Date:

Affirmation:

Who or what inspired you today?

Goals:

Business   Personal   Weekly

Weekly Quote:

I wrote this book to inspire and motivate you to jumpstart your business. If you need more assistance BusinessMomInc™ Can help! We offer Business Management, Marketing, Coaching, and so much more!

For more information please Email:
BusinessMomInc@gmail.Com
or visit our website www.BusinessMomInc.Com

We strive to help the Average Mom become a BUSINESS BEAST!
HOW DO WE DO IT?
Well, we offer support partnerships collaborations and connections within our movement.

Here at Business Mom Inc™ we are taking our business seriously and holding ourselves accountable in fact we believe that success comes a lot easier when you find the right support and resources.

We all have different goals, desires, and ways of leading our lives, we are women trying to be good parents and business owners at the same time and that needs a lot of Support, Resources, and Connections. And that is exactly what you will get here at BUSINESS MOM INC. ™

www.ingramcontent.com/pod-product-compliance
Lightning Source LLC
Chambersburg PA
CBHW041942240526
45473CB00033B/308